THE LONDON
& BLACKWALL
RAILWAY

DOCKLANDS' FIRST RAILWAY

JOHN CHRISTOPHER

AMBERLEY PUBLISHING

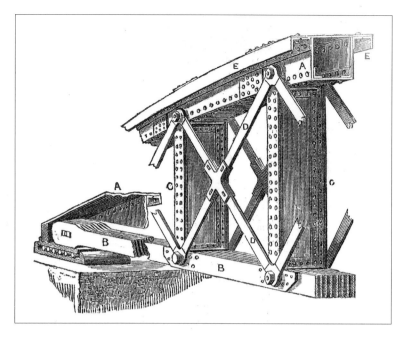

Detail of the Blackwall Extension Railway Bridge which was built to take the line over the Commercial Road, published in *The Illustrated London News*, January 1849.

First published 2013

Amberley Publishing
The Hill, Stroud, Gloucestershire, GL5 4EP
www.amberley-books.com

Copyright © John Christopher, 2013

The right of Author name(s) to be identified as the
Author of this work has been asserted in accordance with
the Copyrights, Designs and Patents Act 1988.

ISBN 978 1 4456 2172 2 (print)
ISBN 978 1 4456 2187 6 (ebook)

British Library Cataloguing in Publication Data.
A catalogue record for this book is available from the
British Library.

Typesetting by Amberley Publishing.
Printed in Great Britain.

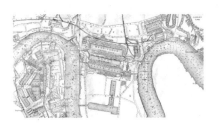

Contents

Opened in 1987, the DLR reused much of the original L&BR viaduct and here two trains pass at Limehouse. *Below*, Engine No. 3 at South Dock station, on the up line of the Millwall Extension Railway.

Docklands

The Port of London is like the human heart with the Thames serving the dual purpose of veins and arteries. Every flood tide gives a new beat of life to Britain and the Empire, for up its grey and muddy waters come the ships of nations with every cargo imaginable.

Britain and the Empire. The term sounds archaic to us now, but this quotation comes not from the nineteenth century, the height of the Victorians' mastery of the world and its trade; it comes instead from a slim volume – *The Port of London* – published in 1947. Speaking with unquestioned confidence, following the rigours of the Second World War, the writer looks to a future for the port that appeared to be stable and enduring, unaware that in a rapidly changing world this view would be turned on its head within two decades.

The story of London's docks, from inception to their dominance, followed by the rapid decline and subsequent rebirth, fits very conveniently into just two centuries – the nineteenth and twentieth. It also happens to mirror the shifting fortunes of Britain as a major industrial and commercial power, and is interlinked with those of the railways. Unusually, however, it was not the railway that took the leading role in the development of the docks; it was the other way around.

By the latter part of the seventeenth century the wharves and warehouses of the Pool of London – the section of the Thames east of London Bridge, which was the main obstacle preventing tall-masted vessels going further up river – were at bursting point. The system of Legal Quays, instigated during the reign of Elizabeth I, had resulted in widespread corruption and stifled the speedy movement of goods. Hundreds of ships were forced to moor in the middle of the river, sometimes for months on end, as they waited for a berth. It is said that by 1800 there were nearly 2,000 vessels vying for space at any one time in a stretch of water suited for no more than 550. Added to which, some 3,000 barges, used to convey goods from ship to shore, or even to store them for long periods, added to the congestion to the extent that it was sometimes possible to walk from one bank to the other on their decks. This situation also left vessels and their cargoes vulnerable to costly pillaging by organised gangs known as 'River Pirates'.

It wasn't until the 1790s that Parliament finally paid heed to the complaints of the merchants and the ship-owners and considered a number of remedies, including the option of creating wet docks. One proposal was to cut a wide channel straight through the Isle of Dogs, leaving the great loop of the river to serve as docks and, incidentally, cutting out the long journey around the Isle, which was always a tricky operation for sailing ships. Another scheme was to create two parallel docks lying across the Isle of Dogs, from Limehouse to Blackwall, with one for imports and the other for exports. This became the basis of the West India Docks, which were completed in 1802. The following description comes from Black's *London and its Environs*, a guide published in 1863:

> The West India Docks are the most extensive on the river, and perhaps have no equal in the world. They are situated at the bend of the river, opposite Greenwich, called the Isle of Dogs. The Blackwall Railway has a station where passengers can alight. They were commenced in 1800, William Pitt, the minister, laying the first stone, and were finished in two years. Their area is said to be 295 acres. The wall surrounding them is five feet thick. The basins are connected with the river on each side of the bend, that is, both above and below Greenwich. The great import dock has a length of 170 yards [510 ft] and a breadth of 166 [498 ft]: it is capable of containing 250 vessels, each of 300 tons.

Stimulated by the success of the West India Docks, several new companies were formed for the construction of more docks and warehouses: the London Dock at Wapping (1805), the East India Dock at Blackwall (1806), the Regent's Canal Dock or Basin at Limehouse, which is now referred to as the Limehouse Basin (1820), and St Katharine's Dock on the Pool (1828). Over on the south side of the Thames, the Surrey Commercial Docks (1807) consisted of a group of five docks which mostly handled trade with the Scandinavian countries.

Left, congestion on London Bridge as depicted by Gustav Doré. *Above*, plumes of smoke from the iron foundries and shipbuilding yards at Blackwall. *Opposite*: The Millwall Dock under construction, and port plans published by the *Lloyds List* in 1930. (*CMcC*)

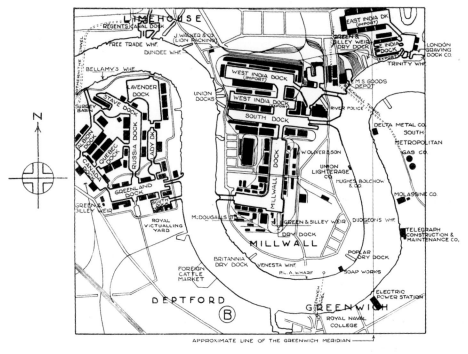

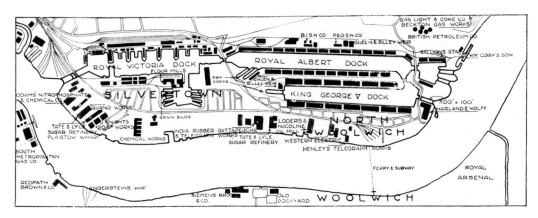

The next spate of dock building saw an extensive area of marshland to the east of Blackwall excavated to create what became known as the 'Royal' docks, which were intended to accommodate the increasingly larger steamships. The Royal Victoria Dock opened for business in 1855. It was joined by the Royal Albert Dock in 1885; this had a basin 1¾ miles long and a water area of 87 acres. Back to the Isle of Dogs and the 'L' shaped Millwall Dock was completed in 1888. The last of the three Royals, the King George V Dock was a relatively late addition in 1921. Built after the coming of the railways, these later docks, from the Royal Victoria onwards, incorporated rail connections in their layout.

Each of the docks had its own character, reflecting its trade in evocative sounds and smells. For Wapping it was tobacco; then there were the heady fumes of the wine and brandy combined with cinnamon and nutmeg at St Katharine's and the London Dock; the rum of the West India Dock; the black coal barges at Poplar; plus sugar, bananas and the sweet sap of pine permeating the air on the Isle of Dogs; and finally there was the meat and dairy produce of the Royals. We can only imagine what it must have been like, this lost landscape that has been recycled, reshaped and reborn.

Shipbuilding

In addition to the docks this part of the Thames, especially on the periphery of the Isle of Dogs, was also an important centre for shipbuilding and it attracted thousands of workers to the area. It was at the Napier Yard in Millwall that Isambard Kingdom Brunel's colossal iron ship, the *Great Eastern*, stubbornly took to the waters in January 1858. (You can still see a section of original timber launch-way which has been uncovered at this location.) The construction of large iron ships also took place at the Thames Iron Works, on the Blackwall side, and this continued well into the first decades of the twentieth century, with the launch of HMS *Thunderer* taking place in February 1911.

Opposite: Shipbuilding on the Isle of Dogs. *Top*, Brunel's *Great Eastern* under construction at Millwall in 1857. *Centre*, launch of the screw-ship *Himilaya* at Blackwall in 1853. *Bottom*, continuing into the twentieth century, the launch of HMS *Thunderer* in 1911 at the Thames Iron Works at Blackwall. (*CMcC*)

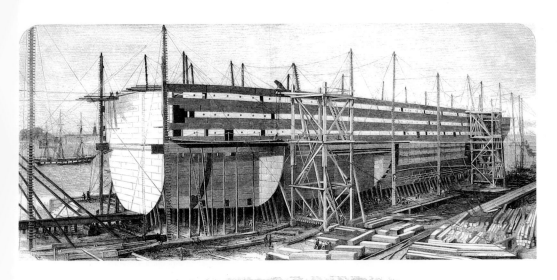

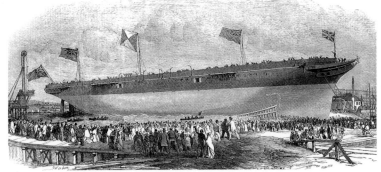

Launch of H.M.S. Thunderer. 5.

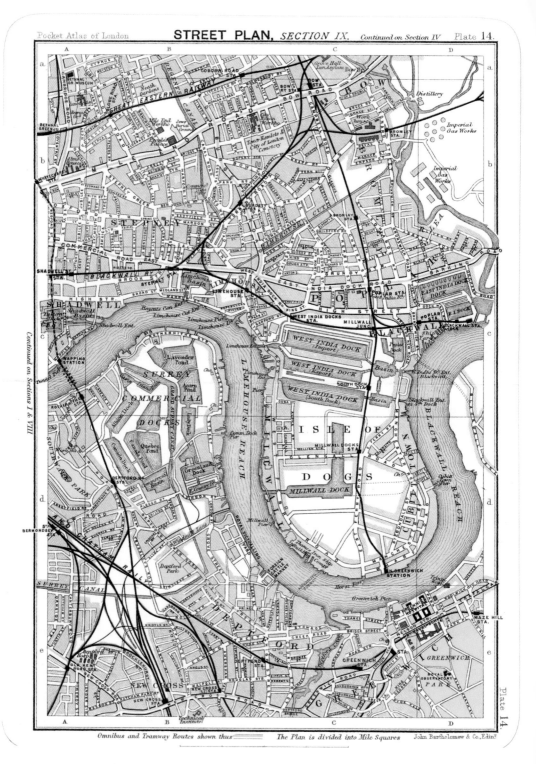

Map from *Bartholomew's Street Atlas*, showing the railways *c.* 1900. The London to Blackwall line runs left to right, with the triangle at Stepney formed by the extension to Bow and the Limehouse Curve.

A Commercial Railway

At the beginning of the nineteenth century, the Commercial Road in London's East End was the main thoroughfare linking the City with the newly completed East and West India Docks. To deal with the consequent increase in traffic, the first scheme for a railway along this route entailed laying rails onto the road itself to create a horse-drawn or, possibly, cable-hauled tramway. Proposed in 1825, this idea was rejected by Parliament three years later. As an alternative a stone tramway was constructed on the Commercial Road and this consisted of granite slabs set into the roadway itself. Because the stones were flat and without metal rails they could accommodate any conventional horse-drawn vehicle provided that its wheels were set at the right distance apart – an early example of the importance of having compatible gauges. One of the engineers responsible for this stone tramway was George Parker Bidder and his name will crop up again.

By the 1830s the success of newly-built steam railways elsewhere in the country created interest in an East London rail link to the docks, and in the spring of 1836 Parliament was faced with two alternative proposals. There was the 'northern scheme' – officially the London and Blackwall and Steam Navigation Depot – which envisaged a railway line running a little to the north of Commercial Road, commencing at Leadenhall Street within the City and curving to the north-east before heading in a straight line as far as Lea Rise, north of the East India Dock. From this line branches would spring off to connect with the West India Docks, the East India Dock and also to Blackwall. The scheme's engineer was Robert Stephenson no less, who intended that the railway would be hidden from view by sinking it within a brick-lined cutting 30 feet wide and 12 feet deep. However, this idea was generally not well received.

The other 'southern scheme' – the Commercial Railway – entailed a line going from East India House, again within the City walls, following a course south of Commercial Road, this time to pass around the top of what was then known as the Regents Canal Basin (later to become the Limehouse Basin) and along the northern edge of the West India Docks direct to Blackwall. Confusingly, this route had originally been surveyed by the Stephensons, father and son, before they had jumped ship to support the northern scheme, leaving the Commercial Railway in the hands of John Rennie (junior). His engineering father had been responsible for the construction of the East and West India Docks.

For both schemes the Blackwall connection was a key element as the Brunswick Wharf, on the curve of the Thames at Blackwall on the eastern tip of the great 'U' looping around the Isle of Dogs, could greatly alleviate some of the congestion of river traffic pushing further upstream to the Pool of London and St Katharine's Docks. In addition, the water at Blackwall was deep enough to accommodate larger vessels capable of going either to the Continent or even further afield, with some taking emigrants to far-flung parts of the British Empire.

After examining the two schemes, Parliament came down on the side of the southern route and granted:

> An Act for making a Railway from the Minories to Blackwall, with Branches, to be called 'The Commercial Railway' dated 28 July 1836 in the reign of William IV.

Note, however, the Bill states that the line was to start at Minories, not at East India House as originally proposed. This was because the Corporation had refused permission for a station to be built within the City walls. The site at Minories, on the road running northwards from the Tower of London, and hence just outside of the City, was the nearest they could get.

With the southern scheme approved, the former rival factions joined forces and by mutual agreement both Robert Stephenson and John Rennie stood aside to make way for the appointment of a more acceptably neutral engineer. Accordingly it was William Cubitt who was tasked with building the line, and at the first meeting of the board of directors for the newly formed company he outlined his plan:

> Commencing at a height of clear eighteen feet, the railway crosses, without interruption, the road leading to Brunswick Hotel and Wharf, and proceeds on arches in the form of an elevated viaduct, with a gradual rise of 1 in 440, or twelve feet per mile, over fields, streets, lanes, roads, canals and water courses, without interfering with any; and by means of easy and unobjectionable curves, avoiding all property of a very valuable or peculiar description, it passes through a neighbourhood consisting of houses of the lowest and poorest description to its terminus at Minories.

Although Parliamentary assent empowered a railway company to purchase properties on an intended route, Cubbitt's viaduct simplified the issue of crossing any roads or waterways while cannily avoiding the expense of buying out the well-to-do – albeit with scant consideration to the rights or wishes of the poorer inhabitants. As the Victorian railway network spread its tendrils, this disregard for the lower strata in society became a commonplace. For many Londoners the coming of the railways saw their communities physically sliced in two, and many thousands of people were displaced in the process. Perhaps this is what prompted Cubitt to suggest that some of the railway arches on the proposed line could be 'converted into more cleanly and comfortable dwellings than four-fifths of those which will have to be taken down'. Or perhaps his apparent philanthropic inclination was only a thinly disguised bid to increase revenue for the company. (Incidentally, the L&BR was not the first line in the capital to be built on a string of viaducts. On the south side of the Thames, the London & Chatham Railway, opened in 1836, was carried on a long brick viaduct consisting of 878 brick arches – a feat of construction that caused a temporary shortage of bricks in the capital.)

It was also William Cubitt who stipulated that the Commercial Railway should be built to a gauge wider than the more prevalent 4 feet 8½ inches which was gaining ground elsewhere,

Robert Stephenson was closely involved with the L&BR. Stephenson had previously employed the rope-hauled system to take the early trains from Euston, shown *below*, up the Camden Incline. The illustration, *right*, shows the tall chimneys of the Camden winding houses. You can see the rope between the rails.

Minories station on the L&BR, with the top of the rope drums protruding at track level. The man on the right is operating a brake to regulate tension on the cable. Note the brakeman travelling at the rear of the train. You can just see the Cook-Wheatstone electric telegraph to the far left.

"CLIPPER" OF THE BLACKWALL RAILWAY.

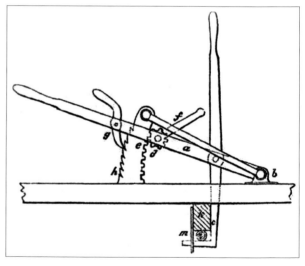

Above, a drawing of the grasping mechanism which held the carriages to the rope.

Left: The 'Clipper' worked from a chamber below the tracks to ensure that the cable was wound in the correct manner.

14

although it was far too early to describe this as the 'standard gauge'. In fairness, it was not unusual for early railways to be built in isolation, without a view to joining up with other lines in the future, and as a result there were several instances of differing gauges in parts of the country. This choice of a gauge, which was a little over 5 feet wide, would prove to be especially irksome for the Stephensons, who maintained a continuing involvement with the London to Blackwall line. Nationally, their 4 feet 8½ inch gauge – admittedly adopted from the existing rails used in the north-eastern collieries – was gaining ground. But before long there would be a conflict with Isambard Kingdom Brunel's broader gauge of just over 7 feet which was dominating in the west and south-west of the country. As the disparate railway schemes grew into a cohesive network the problem of conflicting gauges inevitably caused disruption wherever they met, and the two engineers found themselves drawn into what became known as the 'Battle of the Gauges'. On a personal level Stephenson and Brunel were the closest of friends, but the issue of gauge was perhaps their greatest professional disagreement, although not by any means the only one. The matter was eventually decided by a Parliamentary Commission in 1846 which found in favour of the Stephensons, and their gauge was adopted as the so-called 'standard'. It was chosen not for reasons of technical superiority, but because of sheer weight of numbers, or rather length of rails, in terms of the territory already covered.

If the question of gauge hadn't already set the Commercial Railway apart from the others, the method of traction certainly did. George Parker Bidder, the engineer who had proposed the stone tramway earlier, recommended that the railway line should be worked by a system of ropes or cables hauled by stationary engines, rather than conventional steam locomotives. This would, he argued, greatly alleviate the hazard of fires being started by stray sparks from the locos. Interestingly, the Act of Parliament had not prescribed a particular form of traction to be adopted, only stating that 'locomotives or other engines' could be used. If it happened to be locomotives then they would require approval from the Commissioners of Woods to ensure that proper precautions were taken to minimise the danger of fire caused by stray sparks and cinders. Accordingly, it was stipulated that screened hoods or covers of wire gauze would need to be fitted at the top of the chimney stacks. The concern was not confined to the risk to buildings in the immediate vicinity of the proposed railway, but also to the throng of wooden sailing vessels crammed into the docks and their cargoes. Fire hazard aside, at this early stage in the development of Britain's railways the steam locomotive was still a relatively untried innovation. It had yet to prove itself in terms of reliability and was far from asserting its dominance as the only form of traction for every situation. For example, in 1825 one commentator – Nicholas Woods in *A Practical Treatise on Railroads* – cautioned that locomotives were unlikely to ever exceed twelve or more miles per hour.

The rope haulage proposal found an unlikely supporter in the form of the Stephensons. History portrays them as the champions of the locomotive and so it seems highly incongruous that they should come down on the side of cable haulage for this relatively short line to Blackwall. But the choice was not without precedence. On the Stephensons' first railway, the Stockton & Darlington, the early locomotives had proved to be so unreliable that the railway company considered abandoning them in favour of horses. When this line opened in 1826, to take coal from the pits in north-west Durham to the Tyne at Jarrow, locomotives were used only to haul the coal wagons at either end of the line while the inclines encountered in the middle section were worked by cable. Even the Liverpool & Manchester Railway, when it opened, featured cable haulage on the 1 in 48 incline down to the dockside at Liverpool, and this method had been on the cards for the 1 in 100 grades at Rainhill if the performance of the Stephensons' *Rocket* at the historic 'trials' had not demonstrated that steam locomotives were up to the job.

As late as 1837, when the capital's first major railway terminus had opened at Euston for the London & Birmingham Railway, Robert Stephenson installed stationary steam-driven winches at the top of the Camden incline as he considered the current locomotives to be incapable of pulling heavily laden trains up the 1¼-mile-long slope. Departing trains had to be pushed out of Euston station to the point where the rope could be attached and were then hauled up the incline. On the way down to Euston, men known as 'bankriders' rode on the trains to manipulate the brakes. This rope-hauled system lasted until 1844, but even afterwards the early trains departing from Euston required assistance from a second locomotive at the rear.

There are numerous examples of other cable-hauled railways, such as the Cromford & High Peak Railway opened in Derbyshire in 1831, and to this day San Francisco's iconic cable cars 'clang, clang, clang' up and down the city's undulating hillsides. But almost without exception all of these examples involve some degree of incline, usually a steep one at that, which makes the L&BR all the more unusual.

So what were the main advantages of rope hauling? In addition to the reduced fire risk, the quiet engine-less trains were thought to be less intrusive to the locals; not frightening the horses, so to speak. This consideration was not only to appease the inhabitants of adjoining houses in the densely populated East End, but may have had more to do with not upsetting the City Corporation, which needed careful coaxing if the rails were ever to penetrate further into the City. Another obvious advantage of the cable system was that it did away with heavy locomotives, thus simplifying the construction of a lighter line.

The Fourpenny Rope

Two pairs of stationary steam engines were installed at either terminus; 400 hp at Minories and 200 hp at Blackwall, the difference in power due to the slight gradient of 1 in 400 falling over the length of the line which favoured the Blackwall end. Those at Minories were built by Maudslay, Sons & Field, with the engine house located beneath the tracks, while the ones at Blackwall were by Barnes & Miller. These engines turned huge 23 ft cable drums to wind in the cable with its train attached. It was important to start the engines gradually to avoid sudden snatching on the rope. This would have been uncomfortable for the passengers and put an unnecessary strain on the rope. Brakes on the drums allowed a controller to maintain the correct tension on the rope behind the moving train, and they could also stop the drum entirely.

There were two pairs of rails, one for each direction of travel, and each had a 7-mile rope running in cast iron sheaves laid in the centre of the track. As the line was approximately 3½ miles long, the remaining 3½ miles of rope on the drum was needed for the return journey. The hefty ropes, with a circumference of 5¾ inches, were manufactured by Huddart & Co. of Limehouse and they were originally of hemp.

A contemporary engraving of the Minories station shows the two cable drums protruding at track level, with an operator clasping the brake on the right-hand platform. His equivalent for the other drum was, of course, at Blackwell. On a platform at the rear of the train, the brakesman is seen operating the rope gripping mechanism. Note, too, what looks like a V-shape protruding up between the tracks in front of the winding mechanism. Located in a room beneath the track, a man known as the 'Clipper' operated a piece of equipment resembling a giant pair of scissors to guide the rope onto the drum without tangles. Like a character from the hellish factories depicted in Fritz Lang's visionary film *Metropolis*, his must have been one of the most arduous tasks imaginable.

The carriages were attached to the rope by means of a gripping mechanism which was operated via levers by a 'Brakesman' riding on a small platform at the end of each carriage. This not only provided a strong grip on the rope but also the means of casting off from it, by removing a pin from the coupling. This was done while the train was still in motion to bring individual carriages at the rear of the train to a standstill at the intermediate stations using the handbrake. The stated advantage of this method was that the passengers arrived at their chosen destination without having to stop the whole train.

The line was officially opened as the London & Blackwall Railway on Saturday 4 July 1840 amid much ceremony, with the Lord Mayor of London riding a special train to Blackwall Wharf in the afternoon to attend a banquet held in the East India Company's warehouse, which had been decked out with flags for the occasion. A report in *The Literary World* stated:

> The Blackwall Railway was opened, experimentally, on Saturday last, by a large party of the Directors and their friends; the Lord Mayor, the Sheriffs, and other public functionaries; when the trip was accomplished in somewhat more than eight minutes! There was a liberal sprinkling of elegantly-dressed ladies, a handsome festival, and, of course, a happy day.

Two of the intermediate stations, Stepney and Shadwell, were not to open until August and October respectively.

Regular passenger services commenced on Monday 6 July, on just one of the tracks at first, followed by the other four weeks later. The charge for a single journey was 6d (pre-decimal pence) for a seat in a First Class carriage, or 3d for a standing space in the smaller Second Class 'Stand-Ups'. This was soon increased to 4d, earning the railway its popular nickname of the 'Fourpenny Rope'. There were four trains every hour and on average the journey time from one end of the line to the other was thirteen minutes, so standing up was no great hardship.

Unfortunately, once in operation the hemp ropes proved to be far from satisfactory. They would develop twists and tended to snap after about a month or so, causing disruptions to the service and also expensive repairs as the recoil was violent enough to damage the trackwork. New ropes with the hemp wound around a metal core helped to alleviate the problem to some extent, but even these were likely to fail after twelve months. There were also some incidents with the cable jamming.

Telegraphic Communications

One major operational challenge was coordinating the hauling of the cable by means of a communicating system between the winching houses. On the incline out of Euston a signal had been conveyed to the engine man at Camden to commence winding via a pneumatic speaking tube which sounded a trumpet. A more suitable alternative for the longer L&BR line was found in the newly-developed electric telegraph. Developed jointly by William Fothergill Cooke and Charles Wheatstone, this consisted of a receiver with a number of magnetic needles that could be moved by electromagnetic coils to point to letters of the alphabet. The system was popular because it was simple to use and required minimal training. It was first proposed for communication between the station at Liverpool and the winding engine house at the top of the incline on the Liverpool & Manchester Railway. In the event, the railway opted for a pneumatic system equipped with whistles. An improved version was demonstrated for the Camden incline, but once again rejected. The first commercial success came when it was installed on a 13-mile section of the Great Western Railway between Paddington and West Drayton in 1838, and was later extended to Slough. The L&BR was equipped with the Cooke-Wheatstone telegraph and it can be seen in the image of the Minories station – *see page 14*. The patents for their electric telegraph were bought by the Electric Telegraph Company and this concern became part of the General Post Office in 1869.

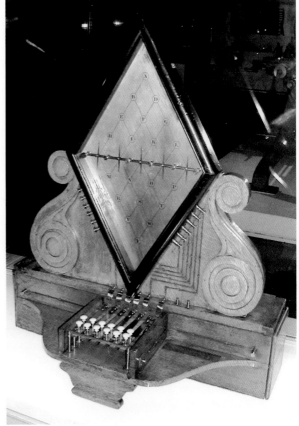

Charles Wheatstone, one of the inventors of the electric telegraph. *Below*, the two-needle apparatus on the GWR, and right an example of the five-needle machine at the Science Museum. (*Jonathan Whiteland*). The first telegraph station opened at Slough on the GWR in 1843, *lower right*.

Fenchurch Street terminus, the 'station in the City', was completed a year after the rest of the line in 1841. The façade is a result of rebuilding work in the 1850s, and is shown here in the 1980s. (*Ben Brooksbank*) The scene inside the station, *c.* 1905. The platforms on the right are for trains taking the line up to Bow, and these trains are showing headboards for Ongar and Southend. The platforms on the left were for the L&BR lines. (*John Alsop*)

Fenchurch Street to Blackwall

The original London to Blackwall line included the following stations, going from west to east: Fenchurch Street, Minories, Leman Street, Cannon Street Road, Shadwell and St Georges East, Stepney East, Limehouse, West India Docks, Poplar, Blackwall. Not all of these were operational right from the beginning, and others were closed during the course of the railway's life. To further complicate matters, in some instances their sites were shifted, and while a number of locations and names are still in use others have been appropriated by the DLR for entirely different stations.

Fenchurch Street

John Betjeman, the renowned lover of railways and architecture, once described Fenchurch Street as a 'delightful hidden old terminus'. But alas, his statement that it 'has been less messed about than any London terminus' no longer holds true. Its old charms have been swept away; the great passenger shed roof – under which Betjeman would depart on a day-return trip on the old London Tilbury & Southend Railway line for afternoon tea beside the sea in Southend – has disappeared, replaced by an office block erected in the 1980s. All that remains is the façade and even that is now pressed in on all sides.

Detail from 1890 map showing the L&BR line from Fenchurch Street, on the left, going as far as West India Docks station, with Blackwell off the edge to the right.

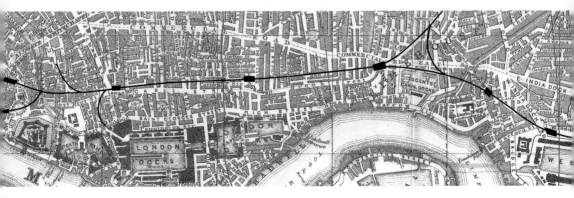

Once described by Sir John Betjeman as a 'delightful hidden old terminus', the interior of today's Fenchurch Street terminus fails to excite. Photographed in 2013, a Southend train waiting to depart from Platform 3.

The viaduct into Fenchurch Street has been much widened over the years. The original Minories viaduct, *right*, was enclosed to reduce the intrusion of the railway as it came within the hallowed walls of the City, so as to not frighten the horses.

The Minories pub indicates the location of the original station and the winching houses. The doors beneath the viaduct are sometimes described as being relics from the station, but they are more likely to have been part of the Royal Mint Street goods depot.

Tower Gateway sits slightly to the south of the site of the Minories station. This was the western terminus for the DLR until the spur was created to Bank. The platform arrangement has been altered to accommodate a single line with platforms to either side.

Fenchurch Street station was not the terminus for the L&BR when the line opened for business in 1840. That was Minories until the following year, when the short extension westwards into the City was completed. The original Fenchurch Street station building had a simple two-storey frontage. On the ground level it had five entrances, topped by semicircular segmental arches, leading into the booking hall. At either side there were buttressed sections, protruding slightly and surmounted by triangular pediments. The upper windows gave light to the end of the passenger shed, with just the two platforms serving the L&BR accessed by stairways ascending from the booking hall.

Because the new terminus was to the west of the Minories winding gear, incoming trains were released from the rope at Minories to cruise into Fenchurch Street under their own momentum. Outgoing trains needed to be pushed by railway personnel until they began to roll down the slight incline to Minories, where they could be connected to the rope. To placate the City Corporation, the section of line to Minories was entirely enclosed by a wooden structure with a tin roof and sash windows along the sides. This was not, as is sometimes suggested, to contain noises and sparks of steam engines as it would be another eight years before they made an appearance on the line with the opening of the London & Blackwall Extension Railway in 1849 – *see the next section*. An increase in the number of trains coming into Fenchurch Street brought about the rebuilding of the terminus, which was completed in 1853. It now had four platforms beneath an iron and glass roof 300 feet long and with a graceful arched span 101 feet wide.

The new station façade was far grander than its predecessor with eleven bays on the ground floor, each with a tall round-topped window above to bring light into the enlarged concourse. The whole was capped by a wide semi-circular pediment. This is the façade that you can still see today in Fenchurch Place. However, this 'station in the City' hasn't always been greeted with universal approval, as this somewhat acerbic description of the L&BR published in the *Argosy* in 1867 reveals:

No ornament has been wasted on its Fenchurch-street Terminus, to begin with. Half a dozen cabs almost fill the little open space it fronts, and the façade is of the least florid order of Pointless architecture. Space is everywhere economised. Curt notifications of 'No Admittance frown over its narrow egress portals, and through equally cramped ingress doorways, which almost touch the others, the passenger finds his way into booking-offices not much larger than good sized packing-cases ... The steps that lead up to the platforms are dark and narrow. When a train comes in between a couple of platforms, it lies jammed like a tier of ships in dock; and the engine that brought it in has to remain skulking against the buffers until another engine has panted away with the carriages once more. As passengers tumble out of them on one side, passengers tumble into them on the other. There is not much waiting at the Fenchurch-street Terminus.

Arriving under the station's gloomy concrete slab of a roof on a busy weekday, many modern commuters might agree with our Victorian journalist. One final note on Fenchurch Street; it is the only one of London's major termini not on the London Underground network. The nearest Underground station is Tower Hill, two or three streets away.

A hydraulic accumulator tower which powered the wagon hoist to the Royal Mint Street Depot. The hoist building has gone but the tower remains with its faded lettering. (*John Keogh, jv21. com*)

Don't blink or you miss the remains of the Shadwell & St George's East platforms, photographed here in 1982. (*Nick Catford*)

Entrance to the former Shadwell & St George's East station on Shadwell Place, 2007. (*Nick Catford*)

Minories

This was the site of the original terminus when the L&BR opened on 6 July 1840. Close to the Tower of London, the name Minories, coming from the parish and the street, is derived from the Abbey of the Minoresses of St Mary of the Order of St Clare, founded in 1294. Minories station became redundant with the cessation of rope hauling and the arrival of the steam locomotives – *see London & Blackwall Extension Railway*. The stationary winding engines were sold at auction, along with their boilers, and were put to work at the City Corn Mills.

The station officially closed on 24 October 1853. The old station buildings have gone and The Minories pub now occupies an archway on the site. It is also possible to see various entrances beneath the viaduct, although these may have been associated with the goods depot as the lower levels were later incorporated in the Mint Street Goods Depot, part of which is now used for parking beside the DLR Tower Gateway terminus, which opened in August 1987. This is no longer the most western point of the DLR as a spur from Royal Mint Street Junction was completed in July 1991 to link up with the Underground and Bank station in the heart of the City.

Heading eastwards out of Tower Gateway, you can't fail to notice a redbrick tower on the south side of the tracks. This is a hydraulic accumulator tower on the site of the former Midland Railway's City Goods Depot, which opened in 1862 and closed in 1949. It supplied hydraulic power for the lifts. On the side facing away from the railway, it is possible to just make out the faded lettering, 'London Midland & Scottish Railway – City Goods Station and Bonded Stores'. Over the years several goods depots and yards sprang off from the main line near Minories, including Mint Street for Great Northern Goods, Goodman's Yard, the City Goods mentioned above, and Haydon Square for London & North Western Railway Goods. Between Minories and Canon Street Road, there was also the Great Eastern Railway Goods.

Leman Street

Located on the east side of Leman Street and north of the aptly named Cable Street, this station was a relative latecomer, opened in June 1877. At first the Board of Trade inspector had delayed the opening on the grounds of safety, and alterations were made to widen the platforms. Our correspondent from the 1867 *Argosy* had previously commented on the inadequacies of the L&BR's smaller stations:

> ... when the passenger has reached the top of the filthy cellar stairs, he find himself in a tiny wooden Dutch over, which can be traversed in half a dozen strides, but which he is afraid to traverse, lest he should knock fellow passengers off the narrow shelf which does duty for a platform.

Leman Street was rebuilt between 1893 and 1896 as part of the widening of the line between Fenchurch Street and Stepney, and brick-built buildings with awnings were erected on both platforms, with a new street level building on the junction of Leman and Cable streets. However, with declining usage the station closed in July 1941 and was demolished in the 1950s. The street level building went the same way during the construction of the DLR in the 1980s.

Looking west from the DLR Limehouse station, the site of the L&BR's Stepney station, where the lines of the London & Blackwall Extension fork off to the right beyond the fence. These are still used by the main line trains going to Fenchurch Street.

Cannon Street Road

A very short lived station, Cannon Street Road opened in August of 1842 and closed six years later at the end of 1848. It was located to the north of the London Docks, which since have been filled in for rebuilding. This section of the L&BR viaduct was demolished during the construction of the DLR.

An account from an 1851 edition of *The Illustrated London News* describes the journey so far:

> Through the windows we had a glimpse of the Tower of London; but soon emerged from the covered way, amid roofs of houses, an ocean of pantiles, and groves of chimneys. We passed the sugar-baking district of Goodman's-fields, the London Docks, Wapping, St George's-in-the-East – a neighbourhood densely crowded with a busy, dingy, working or sea-going population. On the left we passed near Shadwell Church, and also St Mary's Church and schools, recently erected. We next arrived at Stepney Station, and began to breathe more freely, for we had left behind the region of smoke and gigantic chimneys. On the right is the new district church of the parish of Shadwell ...

Shadwell and St Georges East

Opened in October 1840 as Shadwell, the station was rebuilt during the widening of the tracks in 1895 and renamed Shadwell & St George's East in 1900. The platform buildings and down platform were demolished in the 1950s. Today, only the remaining platform on the south side of the track can be glimpsed from a passing train, and at street level the redbrick entrance structure on Shadwell Place has survived and is now in commercial use.

Stepney East (DLR Limehouse)

Opened in 1840 as Stepney station, this later became the junction for the London & Blackwall Extension Railway, which is described in the next section. It was largely rebuilt in 1876 and renamed as Stepney East in 1923. The platforms on the old Fenchurch Street to Blackwall line closed in May 1926. (Today it is known on the DLR as Limehouse and this is the last point where passengers can connect with main line trains coming from Bow on their way into Fenchurch Street.)

To the east of the L&BR's Stepney station, and before reaching Limehouse, the railway viaducts straddle the edge of what is now referred to as the Limehouse Basin. Originally this was called the Regents Canal Docks or Basin and it is where the canal boats met vessels from the Thames, as the trusty *Bradshaw's Descriptive Railway Handbook* of 1863 explains:

> Here begins the Regent's Canal, which after several windings and tunnels through the northern part of London joins the Paddington Canal, and forms an important part of our inland navigation. The pier affords an easy communication with Poplar. What is called the Pool, where all the coal vessels lie, terminates at Limehouse reach.

Incidentally, the octagonal tower seen on the eastern side of the Limehouse Basin has nothing to do with the railway. This is an hydraulic accumulator tower. Built in 1852, a steam engine pumped water to a cylinder at the top of the tower and this powered the cranes beside the basin.

An eastbound train, No. 126, at Limehouse.

Today the Limehouse Basin feels like a marina, but the Limehouse dock had been an important and busy interchange with barges on the Regent's Canal as depicted here by Gustav Doré.

The viaduct at Limehouse and, *left*, the DLR Limehouse station, which straddles the viaduct on the site of the L&BR Stepney station.

A view from the driverless train, heading eastwards through the hoops to Westferry. This is roughly where the L&BR Limehouse station had been.

The site of the original Limehouse station, looking west in 1975 after the tracks had been lifted. (*Nick Catford*)

Continuing on the eastward journey, shortly before reaching DLR Poplar.

This view from the train looking back down the line from the DLR Poplar station shows how the light railway can cope with undulations in the track layout. *Below,* the covered footbridge crossing over the busy Aspen Way to the station.

The eastbound line at DLR Poplar with a glimpse of the depot in the background. The futuristic covered footbridge over Aspen Way is a favourite with photographers, especially at night when it is illuminated.

A rare illustration of an original L&BR station, in this case West India Docks, with the rope-hauled train passing over the viaduct. It was closed in 1926 and no evidence of the station remains.

Limehouse

This is the original Limehouse station and not to be confused with the DLR Limehouse – *see Stepney station*. It was opened in July 1840, on the east side of Three Colt Street, and featured timber platforms built onto the side of the viaduct plus entrance buildings incorporated within the side of the viaduct on both sides. The platforms have gone and the street level buildings remain. From the train the location of the L&BR Limehouse station is easy to identify by the stretch of blue hoops over the track. It closed for passengers in May 1926, but continued in use for freight traffic until 1962, when the Limehouse Curve was taken out of service. This was to the west of the station and formed a link with the London & Blackwall Extension.

West India Docks

No need to guess the location for this one. Opened in July 1840, it had wooden platforms built onto the side of the viaduct with a two-storey structure incorporated within it. It was altered by the Great Eastern Railway in the 1890s, when they also replaced the bridge over the West India Dock Road. The station closed in May 1926 and was demolished in the 1930s. As with Limehouse, it remained in freight service until the closure of the Limehouse Curve.

Beyond the West India Docks station the line comes down from its lofty viaduct and continues eastwards on a gentle incline.

Poplar

Not to be confused with the DLR station of the same name, the first Poplar was in a slight cutting on the west side of Brunswick Road, but only for a very brief period from the opening of the L&BR in 1840 until a new station was opened on the east side of the road in around 1845. This closed in 1926 and all evidence of both sites has been lost beneath the Aspen Way road, which was completed in 1993. The present DLR Poplar is further to the west than the old station, which was roughly where the DLR Blackwall station stands.

Blackwall

Brunswick Quay was built by the East India Dock Company in the 1830s. The eastern portion of the quay was purchased by the L&BR for their terminus and that section of the quay was renamed as Blackwall Pier. Contemporary illustrations of the terminus reveal an imposing two-storey building by William Tite, who had also designed the New Royal Exchange. Built parallel to the wharf, it had a high frontage constructed in brick with Portland stone dressings and a slate roof. On the ground floor there were the usual booking halls, waiting rooms – separate ones for ladies and gentlemen – and toilets.

The building had a low level extension on either side running the length of the train shed. The original stationary engines and winching mechanism for the ropes were located slightly to the west, with an uphill gradient running into the terminus to allow the detached coaches to roll up to the two platforms.

As rail traffic to Blackwall declined, by the early twentieth century the building had fallen into disrepair. The line closed in May 1926 and in the 1930s there were plans to demolish it to make way for a power station. These plans were shelved until after the war and in 1947 the demolition went ahead with the Brunswick Wharf Power Station built on the site. This began generating electricity in 1953, but like many London power stations it in turn became redundant and stopped generating in 1987, coincidentally the year in which the DLR opened. It was partially demolished and downgraded to a sub-station before final closure in 2003. The land is now part of the Virginia Quays residential development and there is no surviving evidence of the old terminus. The DLR Blackwall station is a little further west and the DLR East India is now the nearest to the original site.

Rail Users

At the time of its opening, the L&BR was described in *The Literary World* in the following terms:

> Although it is the shortest, it is one of the most important of the metropolitan lines... It is designated 'The London and Blackwall *Commercial* Railway', the principal object of its construction being the conveyance of merchandise; although its passenger transit will, doubtless, be very considerable.

In fact the passenger traffic proved to be very important to the railway company, and the mix of passengers was as rich as it was unusual. Firstly there were the dock workers and the seamen, then the excited day-trippers who would take the steam packets from Blackwall to Gravesend or Margate, plus countless travellers and even whole families of emigrants heading for other countries. The *Argosy*'s reporter from 1867 offers the following observation:

> The majority of your fellow passengers are sure to be seafaring men, shipping-clerks, emigrants, or people in some way or other connected with the Great Deep or the shallower current of the river ... The

View from Preston's Road bridge in 1962, looking towards the first Poplar station. The line to the right leads to the LMS Dock. Note the tall chimneys of the Brunswick Wharf power station. (*Ben Brooksbank*) *Below*, the DLR Blackwall station is close to the old Poplar site and further west than the L&BR terminus.

Above: The Brunswick Dock, with its distinctive mast house, became part of the East India Docks. *Right*: Contemporary engraving of the rather grand L&BR Blackwall terminus building on Brunswick Wharf. It was demolished after the Second World War to make space for the Brunswick Wharf Power Station, *below*, which in turn has since been demolished.
(*Tim Brown, 2013*)

RETRIBUTION, OR THE GREENWICH DINNER

Lord John Russell. "THIS CAN'T BE WHITEBAIT?"
Lord Palmerston. "OH, YES! YOU WOULD MAKE IT SO LATE IN THE SEASON."

The L&BR attracted a mixed clientele, from the dock workers – as depicted *above* in this scene of a ganger and his men at Millwall Dock published in an 1892 edition of *The Graphic* – to the pleasure seekers catching boats or whitebait.

The taverns of Blackwall and Greenwich were renowned for their fresh whitebait suppers, especially by Cabinet Ministers apparently, causing *Punch* to feature the slippery chaps – the fish that is – in this cartoon.
Below, a Tilbury–Gravesend ferry, operated by the LMS, alongside the Town Pier at Gravesend. Steam packets from Blackwall connected with both Tilbury and Gravesend. (*CMcC*)

conversation bristles with 'shes' and 'hers'. Ships that have sailed or about to sail, ships that have not been heard of, or have just been docked, that were seen coming up the river last night, or brought up this morning in the Hope, ships building, ships repairing, ships loading, form the staple of the talk.

This inadvertent mix of the conspicuously well-to-do traveller rubbing shoulders with the 'hobbydehoy roughs' frequently resulted in opportunistic crimes, such as this 'Robbery on the Blackwall Railway' reported in *The Pictorial Times*:

On Tuesday Information was received at the Bow Street, City, and other police stations, of a foreign gentleman having been robbed of a green leather pocket-book, containing, among other property, numerous Dutch bank notes to the value of nearly £300, whilst travelling, between and nine o'clock, in a second-class carriage of the London & Blackwall Railway. Robberies of this description are now of very frequent occurrence.

But for some travellers it was Blackwall itself that was their destination, as *Bradshaw's* states:

There is a fine pier here, whence packets run to and from Gravesend, in conjunction with the Blackwall railway. Fine views of the shipping of the river, Greenwich, Isle of Dogs and around.

In our globe-hopping age Blackwall seems singularly unimpressive as a place to visit, but for those Victorians who could afford a ticket then the short trip out of the dirty smoke of the city must have been quite magical. Indeed, John Betjeman described Blackwall as 'a palatial terminus on a quay, where the river is so broad that the journey was like one ending on the sea-shore'. And then there was the lure of the fresh whitebait! *Bradshaw's* again:

White-bait dinners form the chief attraction of the taverns adjacent; and here Her Majesty's ministers for the time being regale themselves annually on that fish; the season is from May to the latter end of July, when parliament generally closes for the season.

Such was the notoriety of these ministerial jollies to Blackwall, and also across the river by ferry to Greenwich, that they became symbolic of the tendency among the politicians to prevaricate at the expense of their official duties. As Charles Dickens was prompted to ask:

Why do Cabinet Ministers eat Whitebait? And why do they eat them at the close of the parliamentary session in a tavern at Blackwall or Greenwich? Whitebait, being fish, are cold-blooded animals; but is there on this ground any analogy between them and Cabinet Ministers?

Sadly, the present DLR Blackwall station has little to recommend it – not even a whitebait supper – apart from a fine view across the river of the O_2 dome and the Emirate Airline Thames Cable Car. Opened in June 2012, in time for the London Olympics, the cable car whisks passengers high over the Thames between the Greenwich peninsula and the Royal Docks.

In 1849 the newly completed Blackwall Extension Railway Bridge, crossing over the wide Commercial Road, was heralded by *The Illustrated London News* as 'a remarkable work'. The present bridge, just north of the DLR Limehouse station, is a replacement constructed in the 1890s to cope with the increasingly heavy trains using the railway.

London & Blackwall Extension

The line from Fenchurch Street to Blackwall was only 3½ miles long and by the mid-1840s the L&BR's directors realised that they needed to link up with other railways to become part of a bigger network in order to extend their services, in particular to the north-east side of London.

Their first overtures were made to the Eastern Counties Railway (ECR), with a view to connecting with them via a line going up from Stepney to a junction at Bow. However, the ECR wanted none of it at first, despite the offer of a reciprocal arrangement for their trains to run into the City on L&BR rails. It eventually took the intervention of Parliament to force the cooperation of the ECR and the Stepney to Bow line, known as the London & Blackwall Extension Railway, opened in April 1849 as far as Bow Common Junction initially. Only later was agreement reached for the two companies to run on each other's rails. This laid the foundations for further connections over the ensuing years. The East & West India Docks & Birmingham Junction Railway – thankfully renamed as the more succinct North London Railway (NLR) – commenced services between Islington and Fenchurch Street in 1850. The London, Tilbury & Southend Railway (LT&SR) between Forest Gate and Tilbury Fort opened in 1854, with trains into Fenchurch and Shoreditch. And the North London Railway completed a line between Dalston and Broad Street in 1865.

It was that first branch up to Bow that brought inevitable changes to the way in which the L&BR operated. The rope system was replaced by conventional locomotives and the 5 foot gauge was reduced to the standard 4 feet 8½ standard gauge to come in line with the other companies. It so happened that the ECR had also been built to a 5 foot gauge, but had already made the change to standard gauge a few years earlier in 1845.

Work began to reduce the gauge on the northern of the two tracks on the L&BR line in 1847, with the other changed over the following year. Delays in completing the new bridge over the Commercial Road meant that it was May 1849 before the last rope-hauled trains ran between Fenchurch Street and Blackwall, by which time six locomotives had been supplied by the engineering company of Jones & Potts. These 2-2-2 well-tanks featured 5 ft 6 inch driving wheels and were known as the 'Crewe type'. They were given the names *Stepney*, *Shadwell*, *Blackwall*, *London*, *Bow* and *Thames*.

Two additional locos built by George England & Co., christened *Dwarf* and *Pygmy Giant*, followed. These had smaller driving wheels and weighed only 13 tons, and proved to be unreliable.

Seen from street level, the Blackwall Extension Railway breaks away from the London–Blackwall line immediately west of Stepney, now the DLR Limehouse station. The remains of the old station buildings on the branch line can be seen on the northern side of Commercial Road where it joins Flamborough Street.

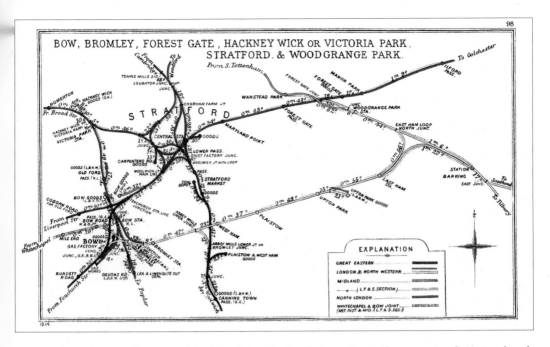

Railway diagram from 1914. The line of the Blackwall Extension Railway coming from Fenchurch Street is on the bottom left corner. By this time the junction at Bow was a gateway to the GER, the L&NWR, the Midland Railway (LT&SR section) and even the Whitechapel & Bow Joint Railway. *Below*, the sweeping curve of the Yorkshire Road viaduct as the line heads off to the north-east.

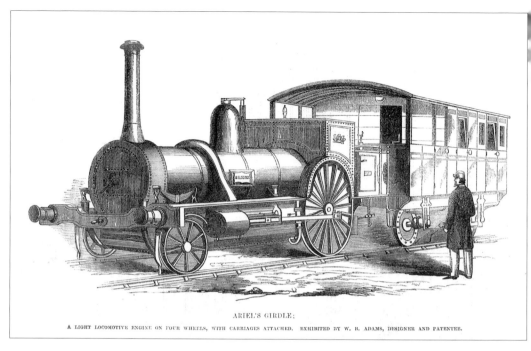

ARIEL'S GIRDLE;

A LIGHT LOCOMOTIVE ENGINE ON FOUR WHEELS, WITH CARRIAGES ATTACHED. EXHIBITED BY W. B. ADAMS, DESIGNER AND PATENTEE.

The first locomotives introduced on the L&BR were, of necessity, light in design. The illustration comes from the illustrated catalogue for the Great Exhibition of 1851. 'Ariel's Girdle; a light locomotive engine on four wheels, with carriage attached. Exhibited by W. B. Adams, designer and patentee.' However, by the time *Ariel's Girdle* was photographed at the North Greenwich station it was clearly sporting an extra pair of wheels. The vertical pipe at the front is the water inlet.

The Route

A contemporary account, published in *The Illustrated London News* on 15 November 1851, describes the journey to Bow as the train coming from Fenchurch Street approaches Stepney and the bridge:

> On the left, but at some distance from the railway, is seen the square tower of Stepney Church, the mother church of most of the parishes in the eastern part of London. Immediately beneath us on the left is the Commercial-road, leading from Whitechapel to Blackwall, a distance of nearly four miles. Near the junction of the Camden-town and Blackwall Railway the Commercial-road is 80 feet in width, and is crossed by an iron viaduct, called Bow Spring Bridge, designed by L. Clare, Esq., and constructed by Messers. Fox and Henderson, of Birmingham. The reader will perceive that, notwithstanding the great length of the viaduct, and the material of which it is constructed, it has a light and picturesque appearance.

Indeed, the skew bridge was generally much admired and it was described as a 'most remarkable' work at the time of its completion in 1849. It is interesting to note that the bridge had relatively high side panels to screen the trains from the horses in the road below. (The builders of the bridge, Fox & Henderson, are more famously known for constructing the Crystal Palace for 1851's Great Exhibition.) The bridge that you see crossing over Commercial Road nowadays is a later replacement. The L&BR's Stepney East platforms on the Blackwall line are now the site of the DLR Limehouse station. If you take a moment to cross to the busy Commercial Road, you will find the remains of the brick building for the station on Flamborough Street beside the line where it branches north-eastwards towards Bow. The other bridge further east along Commercial Road carried the Limehouse Curve, which was taken out of use in 1962.

Our 1851 journey on the London & Blackwall Extension continues:

> Having crossed the Commerical-road by Bow Spring Bridge, we soon leave the City and Pool of London behind us; and pass through fields to Bow-common, where to the right we have an extensive but distant view of the East India docks; and, beyond them, a view of Surrey and Kentish Hills; on the left, the City of London and Tower Hamlets Cemetery, occupying nearly thirty acres of ground, beautifully disposed, and ornamented with cypress, cedar, and other trees, and most of the graves ornamented with flowers and shrubs. This cemetery, with an adjacent field, containing nearly 140 acres of land, is about to be purchased by the Commissioners appointed by Act of Parliament to regulate the burial-grounds of the metropolis. Beyond the cemetery is seen the extensive buildings of the City of London Union Workhouse, which from its extent and architecture has a palatial appearance.

I can't imagine that the inhabitants of the workhouse cared too much for its architectural qualities. That aside, the train then descended into a deep cutting, and, after passing under the Bow Road, arrived at Bow Station.

> Here the train received passengers; and soon after starting we found ourselves in an open country: on the right the newly-formed Victoria Park; on the left we had an extensive view of the Hackney marshes, terminating with a considerable portion of the well-wooded scenery of Essex.

Because the Blackwall Extension is now used by main line trains, the DLR heads north via the Bromley/Bow line just east of DLR Poplar. This line also provides access to the depot off to the left of this photo. Note the 'drive-thu' train-wash. *Below*, a North London Railway 0-4-2ST crane loco at the Devons Road Depot at Bow, 1937. (*CMcC*)

Our correspondent then continued on their way to Camden Town.

The increase in traffic these new connections brought to the line into Fenchurch Street resulted in the viaduct being widened as far as Stepney in 1856 to accommodate an additional Up line. (It was widened again in the 1890s.) Then in 1866 the Great Eastern Railway, which had absorbed the CER by this time, took control of the L&BR through a 999-year lease. Further inter-connections and services followed over the subsequent years. If you take a look at the junction diagram on page 43 you will see how these opened up all sorts of possibilities for the railway companies.

The L&BR's other extension, the Millwall Extension Railway into the Isle of Dogs, is described in the next section.

No. 28, a 4-4-0 tank engine designed by William Adams for the North London Railway and built at their Bow works in 1868.

A snapshot of the Isle of Dogs: *Above,* a 1930s aerial view looking eastwards with Blackwall towards the top left. *Below,* a PLA post-war map showing the docks and various railway lines, including the Millwall Extension Railway, or at least the course of, running north–south.

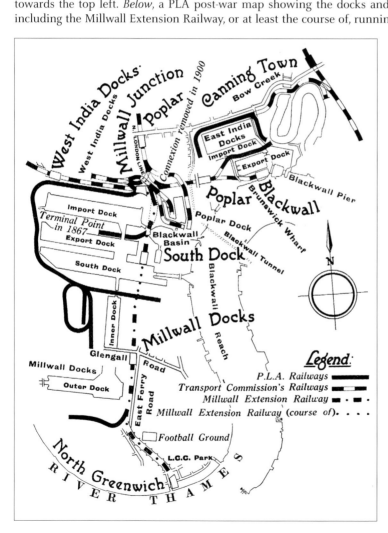

The Millwall Extension Railway

The branch line into the Isle of Dogs was a late addition to the L&BR with the Parliamentary Act for the construction of 'The London, Blackwall & Extension Railway' passed on 19 June 1865, barely seven months before the Great Eastern Railway took over the running of the railway. The plan was to create a new junction between the West India Docks and Poplar stations with a line intersecting the island north to south, in the process improving access to the West India and Millwall docks and linking up with the ferry to Greenwich on the south side of the river.

Even though it was only a single track line, its construction was a slow process, with many complications where it traversed the premises of both the East & West India Dock Company and the Millwall Dock Company, who retained ownership of the land. Furthermore, both of the two intermediate passenger stations were located within the dock area. It was because of this that the dock companies would be closely involved in the working of the new line, together with the GER, and it was placed under the control of a joint committee. But the courtship hadn't been easy and the West India Dock Company had gone out of its way to scupper the scheme as it feared that having the railway coming onto its docks might benefit its competitors.

The Millwall Junction, together with the first part of the line going almost due south, was completed by the end of 1867 as far as the South Docks station. This was located to the east of the gap between the West India Export and South docks. Because the line passed through a narrow gap between the extensive timber yards, the dock company required that horses must draw the carriages over the stretch of track from the Millwall Junction to the Millwall Dock Company's boundary. Only then could steam take over from horsepower, and this precautionary measure confined the locomotives to the southern tip of the Isle until 1880, when the insurance companies relented. The GER purchased three lightweight locomotives to run on the Millwall Extension through the docks with its wooden bridges.

It wasn't until December 1871 that the next section, going to the Millwall Dock station (Glengall Road), was opened for goods and passenger services. This also had a passing loop. The remainder of the line down to North Greenwich station – a somewhat misleading name given that it was actually on the northern bank of the river – finally opened in July 1872. This stretch more closely resembled the main L&BR line at this point as the rails were elevated on a long viaduct, crossing over the Manchester and Wharf roads as far as the riverside station. Those wanting to travel on to Greenwich crossed the river via the steam ferry going from the

Clearly, it was obligatory to lean on a locomotive when being photographed. No. 13, taking on water on the Millwall Extension, was a 0-6-0 saddle built in 1875 by Fox, Walker & Co. The loco had 3 ft 3 inch driving wheels and 12x20 cylinders.

An unidentified North Greenwich train, pausing at the Millwall docks station.

Above, swing bridge in Millwall, looking southward. *Below*, signal box at the reception sidings at Millwall, looking over the course of the Millwall Junction Railway, which had been laid on land owned by the Dock companies in places.

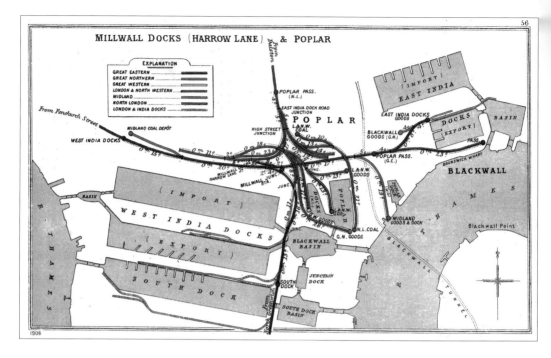

A 1906 railway diagram showing the lines at Poplar junction. Note the proliferation of goods depots for the different railway companies. The Blackwall road tunnel is also shown; this opened in 1897.

GER's pier adjoining the station. The rights to operate the foot ferry were conveyed to the L&BR in 1874 and then taken over by the GER. It was not an insignificant part of the railway's business and at the turn of the century some 1,300,000 passengers made the crossing annually. The journey time between Fenchurch Street and Greenwich, including the river crossing, was said to be a very respectable thirty-six minutes. However, there was no though-working to Fenchurch Street and travellers to and from the Isle of Dogs were obliged to connect with trains on the east-west line.

The trains going between Millwall Junction and North Greenwich ran daily, every quarter of an hour from 7 a.m. until 6 p.m., although with a gap in the service between 11.00 a.m. and 1 p.m. These times indicate that the line was very much concerned with the transportation of the dock workers and not the pleasure-trippers encountered on the Fenchurch to Blackwall service.

New and Old Routes on the Isle of Dogs

In relation to the present DLR line, the Millwall Junction was approximately halfway between the DLR Poplar and DLR Blackwall stations. The line now stems from new 'Delta' junction, which is about a quarter of a mile further to the west of the original one, and cuts straight across what remains of the three West India Docks. It passes through three stations in quick succession: West India Quay immediately after the junction, followed by Canary Wharf and then Heron Quays. These stations seem so close together that there is barely a gap between stops, but this does serve to spread the flow of passengers getting on or off. The line then turns at an angle eastwards, narrowly shaving past the corner of the hotel to arrive at the next station, South Quay, which straddles the top end of the Millwall Inner Dock. The southbound line then executes a sharp right-angle at Marsh Wall to pick up the north–south line of the old railway parallel to East Ferry Road. The elevated DLR Crossharbour station is approximately where the L&BR Millwall Docks station would have been. Continuing south, DLR Mudchute station had no equivalent on the L&BR. (The unusual name comes from the channel which was built to help rid the dock of mud.)

South of Mudchute we come to the point where the original line took to the long viaduct running through Millwall Park – a former home of the football team. When the DLR opened in 1987, the Island Gardens station at Manchester Road was the end of the line, perched on the end of the viaduct itself. But when the line was extended to Greenwich and Lewisham in 1999, this section on the viaduct was closed, along with the original Island Gardens station. Realigned, it now descends beneath ground level immediately south of Mudchute and passes through the replacement Island Gardens to tunnel under the Thames.

Any reference to the Isle of Dogs inevitably raises the question of how this dog got its name. There are several possibilities, but the most frequently repeated one suggests that this is where the king had his hunting kennels, directly opposite the royal residence at Greenwich. Until the nineteenth century the Isle had been an uninhabited marshy area, the Stepney Marsh in fact, until it was drained and a wall erected to keep out the river water. Several windmills were erected on this wall which is how we come to have the 'wall' in Blackwall and the 'mill' in Millwall.

A Cypriot ship, *Anenome*, in the India and Millwall Docks, 1970. Note the piles of timber on the barges. (*CMcC*)

A southbound train approaching Crossharbour station. Perched on stilts beside the Limeharbour and East Ferry roads, Crossharbour is roughly where the old Millwall Docks station was located.

Northbound train departing from Crossharbour station, 2013.
Below, No. 104 coming into Crossharbour.

After it had closed to traffic the North Greenwich station continued to be used for storage. *Below*, happier days with No. 6, a 2-4-0 side tank built by Manning Wardle in 1880, ready for departure from North Greenwich.

Wardle-built 2-4-0 side tank at North Greenwich station, c. 1900. (*Wiki*)
Below, a Blackwall–Fenchurch Street timetable from August 1914, including the trains taking the Millwall extension to North Greenwich.

	eve.	eve.	eve.	eve.	eve.	eve.	eve.	eve.	eve	eve.	eve.	eve.	eve.	eve.	eve.	eve.	eve.
Blackwall ... ...dep.	2 5	2 20	2 35	2 50	3 5	3 20	3 35	3 49	4 5	4 20	4 35	4 50	5 5	5 18	5 35	5 50	6 5	6 20	6 35
Poplar	2 6	2 21	2 36	2 51	3 6	3 21	3 36	3 50	4 6	4 21	4 36	4 51	5 6	5 19	5 36	5 51	6 6	6 21	6 36
North Greenwich ... (Cubitt Town)	1 51	2 6	2 23	2 37	2 51	3 6	3 23	3 37	3 51	4 6	4 23	4 37	4 51	5 6	5 23	5 37	5 51	6 6	6 23
Millwall Docks	1 54	2 9	2 26	2 40	2 54	3 9	3 26	3 40	3 54	4 9	4 26	4 40	4 54	5 9	5 26	5 40	5 54	6 9	6 26
South Dock...	1 57	2 12	2 29	2 43	2 57	3 12	3 29	3 43	3 57	4 12	4 29	4 43	4 57	5 12	5 29	5 43	5 57	6 12	6 29
Millwall Junc. ... arr.	2 0	2 16	2 33	2 46	3 0	3 16	3 33	3 46	4 0	4 16	4 33	4 46	5 0	5 16	5 33	5 46	6 0	6 16	6 33
Millwall Junction ...dep.	2 8	2 23	2 38	2 53	3 8	3 23	3 38	3 52	4 8	4 23	4 38	4 53	5 8	5 21	5 38	5 53	6 8	6 23	6 38
West India Docks	2 10	2 25	2 40	2 55	3 10	3 25	3 40	3 54	4 10	4 25	4 40	4 55	5 10	5 23	5 40	5 55	6 10	6 25	6 40
Limehouse	2 12	2 27	2 42	2 57	3 12	3 27	3 42	3 56	4 12	4 27	4 42	4 57	5 12	5 25	5 42	5 57	6 12	6 27	6 42
Stepney	2 14	2 29	2 44	2 59	3 14	3 29	3 44	3 58	4 14	4 29	4 44	4 59	5 14	5 27	5 44	5 59	6 14	6 29	6 44
Shadwell&St. George's, E.	2 17	2 32	2 47	3 2	3 17	3 32	3 47	4 1	4 17	4 32	4 47	5 2	5 17	5 30	5 47	6 2	6 17	6 32	6 47
Leman Street	2 19	2 34	2 49	3 4	3 19	3 34	3 49	4 3	4 19	4 34	4 49	5 4	5 19	5 32	5 49	6 4	6 19	6 34	6 49
Fenchurch Street arr.	2 21	2 36	2 51	3 6	3 21	3 36	3 51	4 5	4 21	4 36	4 51	5 6	5 21	5 34	5 51	6 6	6 21	6 36	6 51

	eve.	eve.	eve.	eve.		eve.		eve.		eve.		eve.		eve.		eve.	eve.
Blackwall ... ...dep.	6 50	7 4	7 20	7 48	...	8 20	...	8 50	...	9 20	...	9 50	...	1018	...	1050	...	1120	1148
Poplar	6 51	7 5	7 21	7 49	...	8 21	...	8 51	...	9 21	...	9 51	...	1019	...	1051	...	1121	1149
North Greenwich ... (Cubitt Town)	6 45	...	7 7	7 37	...	8 7	...	8 37	...	9 7	...	9 37	...	10 7	...	1037	...	11 7	1137
Millwall Docks	6 48	...	7 10	7 40	...	8 10	...	8 40	...	9 10	...	9 40	...	1010	...	1040	...	1110	1140
South Dock	...	...	...	...	...	...	...	...	...	...	...	...	...	...	...	...	...	...	...
Millwall Junc. ... arr.	6 52	...	7 15	7 45	...	8 15	...	8 45	...	9 15	...	9 45	...	1015	...	1045	...	1115	1145
Millwall Junction ...dep.	6 53	7 7	7 23	7 51	...	8 23	...	8 53	...	9 23	...	9 53	...	1021	...	1053	...	1123	1151
West India Docks	6 55	7 9	7 25	7 53	...	8 25	...	8 55	...	9 25	...	9 55	...	1023	...	1055	...	1125	1153
Limehouse	6 57	7 11	7 27	7 55	...	8 27	...	8 57	...	9 27	...	9 57	...	1025	...	1057	...	1127	1155
Stepney	6 59	7 13	7 29	7 57	...	8 29	...	8 59	...	9 29	...	9 59	...	1027	...	1059	...	1129	1157
Shadwell&St. George's, E.	7 2	7 16	7 32	8 0	...	8 32	...	9 2	...	9 32	...	10 2	..	1030	...	11 2	...	1132	12 0
Leman Street	7 4	7 18	7 34	8 2	...	8 34	...	9 4	...	9 34	...	10 4	..	1032	...	11 4	...	1134	12 2
Fenchurch Street arr.	7 5	7 20	7 36	8 4	...	8 36	...	9 6	...	9 36	...	10 6	...	1034	...	11 6	...	1136	12 4

On Week Days, South Dock Station is closed at 6.29 p.m. and entirely on Sundays.

The Free Tunnel for Foot Passengers between North Greenwich (Cubitt Town) and Greenwich is open day and night. The northern entrance to the Tunnel is near to North Greenwich Station.

THROUGH TICKETS are issued between South Dock, Millwall Docks, and North Greenwich on the one hand, and on the other hand, all Stations on the Blackwall Line, Fenchurch Street to Blackwall and Bow Road inclusive; Stratford and all Stations to Palace Gates, Southend-on-Sea, Burnham-on-Crouch, and Southminster. Stations on the East London Line via Shadwell, Stations on the Midland Railway (London Tilbury and Southend Section), including Gravesend, via Stepney.　　*a* Saturdays only.　　*b* Not on Saturdays.

The southbound train begins the descent just to the south of Mudchute station. *Below,* the truncated Mudchute viaduct, which originally crossed over the road to the North Greenwich station.

A fine survivor, the Mudchute viaduct strides across the park. *Below,* the rebuilt DLR Island Gardens station. The towers are ventilation shafts for the tunnel which continues southwards under the Thames.

LMS open wagons being loaded from a hopper at Millwall Docks

Above: Millwall Junction looking east. The DLR going through Poplar takes the line of the tracks to the left, while those on the right have disappeared under the Aspen Way road.

Left, a BTH Type 1 diesel-electric stands in the closed Millwall Junction, with the docks in the background. (*Tony Powell*)

Decline and Rebirth as the DLR

By the first decades of the twentieth century the L&BR's passenger numbers were falling. To some extent this decline was a result of the railway's own success, especially through its connections via other lines travelling to North Woolwich or Gallions on the eastern side of the Royal Docks rather than to Blackwall to catch the boats. For the Millwall Extension Railway there were other factors. The line had earned considerable revenue from supporters travelling to the Millwall Football Club and on match days it was customary to increase the number of carriages per train. The club had several homes over the course of the years, starting with a patch of waste ground at Glengall Road before moving to a site by the East Ferry Road. Then, in September 1901 the club was required to vacate the land as it was needed for the docks, and it moved to North Greenwich. An even greater blow came in 1910 when the football club moved off the Isle of Dogs to a new ground at New Cross.

The Millwall line also experienced an abrupt drop among the dockers travelling to work when the Greenwich Foot Tunnel opened to the public on 4 August 1902. Prior to that point the volume of cross-river traffic had amounted to 1.3 million people annually, but with the opening of the tunnel the Greenwich ferries had become superfluous and they were withdrawn only months later. The GER received £8,000 in compensation.

Things continued to go from bad to worse for the old railway and during the First World War the GER instigated several station closures as more of their workforce went to fight. Leman Street and Shadwell & St Georges East closed in May 1916 and train services on the L&BR routes were reduced. The usage of these minor stations had been declining anyway, and after the war the motor cars and omnibuses began to make further inroads. Sir John Betjeman recalled this time on the railway in *First and Last Loves*:

Those frequent and quite empty trains of the Blackwall Railway ran from a special platform at Fenchurch Street. I remember them well. Like stage coaches they rumbled slowly past East-End chimney pots, wharves and shipping, stopping at black and empty stations, till they came to a final halt at Blackwall. When one emerged there was nothing to see but a cobbled quay and a vast stretch of windswept water.

1963: A PLA diesel shunter hauls wagons out of the West India Docks. *Below*, a view of Millwall Junction taken from the footbridge going from Harrow Lane to the West India Docks, with the L&BR tracks in the foreground. (*Tony Powell*)

There were significant changes to the structure of the nation's railways with the passing of the 1921 Railways Act, reorganising the many companies in to the 'Big Four'. As a result the L&BR and the GER became part of the London & North Eastern Railway on 1 January 1923.

On the Isle of Dogs, the Millwall Extension suffered further indignities in its twilight years. The three passenger locomotives had become worn out after forty years in service and seeking an alternative, the newly-formed Port of London Authority (PLA) brought in three steam rail-cars which had been discarded by the Great Western Railway. These were entirely unsuited to the conditions on the Isle. They were too heavy, requiring the bridges to be strengthened, and they were patently too long to cope with the sharp curves and in trial runs they damaged the rail-side equipment. The rail-cars were not in operation for long as the Millwall Extension Railway was scheduled to close on 30 June 1926. In the event, it ceased operation even earlier, on 4 May, when pickets taking part in the General Strike intercepted the railwaymen at the dock gates.

The fate of the former L&BL lines remained inexorably linked with the fortunes of the docks they were built to serve. As we have seen in the introduction to this book, the futures of London's docks seemed so secure in the post-war years, even after the battering they received from the Luftwaffe in the Second World War. But when the end came, it came swiftly and from an unanticipated source. During the 1960s the whole business of moving goods by sea, and by road or rail for that matter, was turned on its head by the introduction of containerisation. Suddenly the time taken to unload a ship's cargo went from several days to just a few hours. Furthermore, containers were secure and could be handled in open docks; they could also be stacked one upon another. The old docks were no longer needed. The East India Dock closed in 1967, followed by the London Dock and St Katharine's Dock two years later. The West India Docks survived until 1980, and the three Royals closed the following year.

By the 1960s only the occasional goods trains were using what was left of the old L&BR line, and in 1966 the remainder of the line, including the Millwall extension, was officially abandoned.

The Docklands Light Railway
As valuable building land the speed of the Dockland's redevelopment, especially within the Canary Wharf area at the northern part of the Isle of Dogs, has been bewildering. What had once been a forest of ship's masts was replaced by towering concrete, steel and glass office blocks to house the banks and financial institutions.

The London Docklands Development Corporation recognised the requirement for a public transport system to serve the former docklands area and to stimulate regeneration. It came in the form of the Docklands Light Railway.

Constructed between 1985 and 1987, the DLR was officially opened by the Queen on 30 July 1987, with passenger operations commencing a month later. In essence the DLR is an elevated tramway and the initial routes connected Tower Gateway, built beside the old Minories station site, Stratford to the north-east, and the Island Gardens station at the southern tip of the Isle of Dogs. These three branches totalled 8 miles in length and had fifteen stations. For several of these stations the DLR adopted many of the original station names, although to confuse anyone

Above, the north entrance to the Greenwich Foot Tunnel, which opened on 4 August 1902, causing the cessation of the GER's ferry service to Greenwich.

Left, the Iranian *Sharman* at the New Fresh Wharf in the late 1960s, the twilight years for London's docks. (*CMcC*)

Below: The gates of the East India Dock locked against striking workers, *c.* 1910. In May 1926 the General Strike brought passenger services on the L&BR to a premature end. (*LoC*)

with an interest in the old L&BR some names were swapped around or applied to stations in entirely new locations. A prime example is Stepney East, which became the DLR's Limehouse, not be confused with the old Limehouse which had closed in 1926. *See the previous chapters and Appendix 1: L&BR Stations.* Significantly, much of the DLR followed the line of the original L&BR, reusing the brick viaducts, and elsewhere new stretches were elevated in a way that captures the spirit of the L&BR. As previously mentioned, the major deviation was with the location of the junction going south into the Isle of Dogs, and also the route to Bow, which branches off on the eastern side of Poplar on the former North London line.

Since its opening in 1987, the DLR has seen a number of major improvements and extensions. The first phase, from 1991–94, saw the extension via a tunnel into Bank to improve accessibility within the City, as well as the expansion of Canary Wharf from a small 'wayside' station to a larger complex with six platforms protected from the weather by a spectacular glass roof. An additional branch was opened in 1994, going from Polar to Beckton via Canning Town.

The second phase saw the construction of a tunnel under the Thames to create an extension to Greenwich, Deptford and Lewisham. This opened in December 1999. As a result, the line south of Mudchute descended below ground, with a new subsurface station constructed at Island Gardens.

Between 2004 and 2009 the third phase of extensions and enhancements included an eastward branch, roughly following the route of the former Eastern Counties & Thames Junction Railway on the south side of the Royal Docks, going from Canning Town via London City Airport to King George V. And a further extension under the Thames to Woolwich Arsenal was opened by Boris Johnson, Mayor of London, on 12 January 2009. At the other end of the line the Tower Gateway station was reconstructed, with the previous twin tracks replaced by a single track with platforms to either side.

Since then we have seen upgrading to allow for three-car trains to increase capacity, and as part of the funding for the 2012 Olympic Games a line was opened from Canning Town to Stratford and Stratford International on the former North London line. This opened in 2011 along with a substantial multi-level junction at Canning Town to enable trains from Bank/Poplar and from Stratford International to run to either of the eastern termini at Beckton and Woolwich Arsenal.

The DLR system now has 25 miles of track and forty-five stations, mostly unmanned, with six branches – *see map on page 67*. Several further extensions and enhancements are either under way or being considered. These include going westwards from Bank across London to St Pancras and Euston, eastwards from Gallions as far as Dagenham Dock, and southwards from Lewisham to Catford or possibly to Forest Hill.

Right from the beginning usage of the DLR has exceeded expectations, with 17 million passengers in the first year rising to more than 80 million in 2012. Due to this success, similar light railway schemes are under consideration, including plans for the North and West London Light Railway.

DLR Rolling Stock
Although the trains on the new light railway look more like articulated buses, technically they are termed as high-floor articulated Electrical Multiple Units (EMUs). They are operated on

DLR rolling stock; No. 02 wears the early blue with red livery at Canary Wharf. (*Previnnk*) *Below, the latest version, 2013.*

a fully automated computer-controlled system, without a driver. A Passenger Service Agent rides on each train and he/she is responsible for checking tickets, making announcements and controlling the doors. In some situations they can take control of a train using controls concealed within a console at the front of the train.

When it opened in 1987 the DLR had a fleet of just eleven vehicles, with another ten added the following year. These were replaced in 1991 by seventy new vehicles to cover the extended network. Another twenty-four were added for the London City Airport extension and the DLR fleet had grown to eighty-four by 2008, when refurbishment and new branding was carried out. A further fifty-five three-car trains were ordered in 2007 to run between Bank and Lewisham and also on the enhanced Olympics run to and from Stratford International.

There have been three different main types of rolling stock; however, only the B90/B92/B2K and the B07 remain in service, with the early P86/P89 stock having been sold to a German operator.

Each car is 92 ft long, has four doors on each side and seats seventy people with standing spaces bringing the total capacity to 284.

There are two operating and maintenance depots. One is at Poplar, accessed from the Stratford line to the east of Poplar station, and a more recent and larger depot opened in 1999 on the site of the former Beckton Gas Works. This is accessed via a spur to the north-east of Gallions Reach. (*See page 92.*)

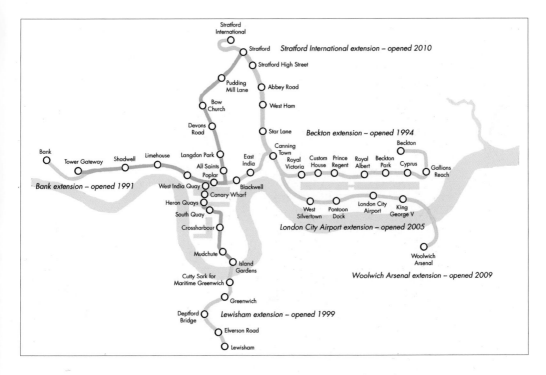

Map of the DLR network showing the various extensions. More are planned.

West India Quay with entrance from beneath the line. *Below*: The Delta Junction, as it is known, has been upgraded to take the heavier three-car trains.

The station at West India Quay seems especially high. *Below*, Immediately south of the station, the bridge over the West India dock leading to Canary Wharf.

Two views of the South Quay station. *Above*, looking west with No. 140 pulling up at the southbound platform, and, *below*, 105 heading off to Crossharbour.

South Quay station spans the top end of the Millwall Inner Dock. It opened in 1987 as a standard Phase 1 elevated station, but was moved in 2004 to create a longer station to handle the three-car trains. *Below*, the view west showing the marked curvature of the line.

The great glass roof of Canary Wharf station seen from Heron Quays. *Below*, interior view of Canary Wharf. Because of delays it opened in 1991, several years after the rest of the line.

Pillars of light: The lofty glass roof at Canary Wharf imbues it with some of the cathedral-like qualities of a classic railway station with a cascade of long shadows.

A northbound train waits to depart from Heron Quays. *Below*, the view northwards to Canary Wharf. The stations are surprisingly close together on this section of the line.

An incoming train from Heron Quays winds its way among Canary Wharf's six platforms. *Below,* the view from a southbound train approaching Canary Wharf.

Two trains pass at Crossharbour station. *Below,* the Limehouse Viaduct.

An eastbound train arriving at Blackwall. *Below*, No.13 waiting at Canary Wharf.

A train awaiting passengers at Canary Wharf. *Below*, riding the L&BR viaduct, one of the finest views of the DLR is across the Limehouse Basin

The Poplar depot seen from the station platform. *Below*, this view of the eastern side of the depot is taken from a train. The DLR has two depots, with a larger one built on the site of the old Beckton gas works.

British steamer *Benmhor* at the India and Millwall Docks in 1970. (*CMcC*)

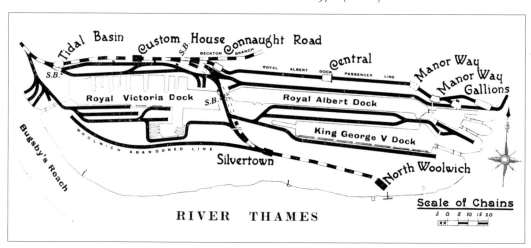

The PLA map from the 1950s shows the 'Royal' group of docks to the east of Blackwall. Note the Woolwich Abandoned Line, which was cut off by the entrance to the Royal Victoria Dock, which opened in 1855. The rail line had to be diverted around the north of the docks to reach North Woolwich. The Royal Albert dock opened in 1880, followed by the King George V Dock, which was completed in 1921. Gallions station is on the far right, with the passenger line to it running across the top of the map.

Other Dockland Railways

In 1860, the first railway to reach one of the docks was a branch from the L&BR. This curved southward from a junction near Leman Street station and went to the Smithfield depot and wool warehouses at London Dock, but it did not extend into the dock itself. (*See the map on page 21.*)

The first fully rail-connected dock was the Victoria Dock – the first of the Royals – which was completed in 1855. In fact, a railway already crossed the site before the construction of the dock. Back in 1845 the North Woolwich Railway Company had been authorised to make a line from the Eastern Counties & Thames Junction Railway to North Woolwich. This opened in June 1847, by which time the line had come under the control of the Eastern Counties Railway. (later to become part of the Great Eastern Railway). In its original position, running parallel to the river on the south side of the dock, the line would have obstructed vessels passing through the new dock entrance and it was diverted further inland to go around the northern edge of the dock. The section of track cut off and left behind became known as the Woolwich Abandoned Line. A second alteration to the layout was required with the construction of the Royal Albert Dock (completed in 1885), this time through a 1,800 ft tunnel passing beneath the canal at the junction between the two docks.

When completed, the Royal docks formed the largest area of impounded dock water in the world, with a wide range of cargoes passing through them including meat, grain, dairy produce, tobacco and motor vehicles. Victoria Dock was initially provided with chilled storage facilities for up to 3,200 sheep carcases, and this was later increased to 13,000 tons of refrigerated meat in the main storehouse on the north side of the Albert Dock. As a result, it became one of the most important commodities handled by the docks' internal rail system.

The process of sorting and checking the rail-borne traffic in and out of the docks was carried out at the Exchange Sidings, the most extensive dock-side railway yard in the country. This was the interchange point between the dock's railways and the external lines.

On the Isle of Dogs

A system of horse-drawn tramways had been laid down at the outset at the Millwall Dock Company's docks, and this was extended to the West India Docks. In the cramped conditions, this layout featured numerous sharp curves – not a problem with horse-power – but when steam

The vast exchange siding for the Royal Docks, viewed from a footbridge. This is the point where the dock railways met the incoming lines. *Below*, loaded meat vans leaving Z shed at the Royal Victoria Dock.

was introduced it was found that six-wheelers took a disproportionate strain on their axles, wheels and connecting rods, and four-wheels became the norm. When a new entrance lock leading from Blackwall Reach into the South West India Dock was opened to shipping in 1929, the dock railway had to be diverted to the west side of the docks to avoid the introduction of swing-bridges. On the Isle the marshalling and dispatch of trains was not confined to a single area as with the Royals, and was carried at dispersed locations with direct connections to Poplar Junction for traffic to the Poplar Dock, and via the Millwall Junction to join with the Blackwall line.

At its height, the rail-hauled traffic handled on the Isle amounted to approximately 6,000 tons per month, the main commodities being sugar, hardwoods, grain and bananas, although the import of the latter was curtailed by the Second World War. Huge quantities of grain were handled at Millwall and this was taken by rail to Welwyn Garden City to be turned into breakfast cereals.

Passenger Trains to Tilbury and Gallions

The railways also provided a vital link to the Tilbury Docks, which opened for business in 1882. Constructed on a vast area of wasteland fifteen miles down river towards the Thames Estuary, Tilbury doesn't come within the remit of this book of dockland railways; however, it is of interest as the main rail link was originally on the London, Tilbury & Southend Railway (LT&SR) extending from Bow Junction, and later connected to the GER at Forest Hill. (*See the diagram on page xxx.*) The Riverside Station at Tilbury was formally opened by the Prime Minister, Ramsey MacDonald, on 16 May 1930, and together with the adjoining landing-stage it remained independent of the PLA

The Gallions signal box, *c.* 1908.

A post-war photograph of the 'A' signal box with the bomb-damaged Tidal Basin station on the extreme right. *Below*, a Custom House train at Gallions station.

and was operated by the London Midland & Scottish Railway (LMS). By arrangement with the PLA, special boat trains were able to take passengers direct to the quays where their ships were berthed, including vessels owned by the LMS itself. Each train carried between 250 and 300 passengers plus baggage, with the arrival or departure of a ship typically requiring three or four special trains.

Passenger and goods trains were also operated by the GER to Gallions Reach, located on the Thames to the east of the Royal Docks, where the Gallions Hotel was built to accommodate passengers waiting to join their ships. During the First World War special trains took munitions workers to Gallions, where they went by ferry to Woolwich. The stations at Gallions and Manor Way were rebuilt or altered several times, and in July 1896 the three dock railway passenger locomotives were withdrawn from service, leaving the GER to provide local trains to Custom House and Gallions. Although the line to the Royal Albert Dock and Gallions had seen almost a hundred trains a day at its peak around the turn of the century, by the Second World War demand had fallen and bomb damage to the line brought the passenger services to an end.

The Port of London Authority

On 31 March 1909 the assets of the dock companies were vested in a single body, the Port of London Authority, which had responsibility for the operation of the main five docks groups, the London and St Katharine's, the Surrey Commercial, the East/West India and Millwall, the Royals and Tilbury. This, of course, included the operation of the railways on dock property. It is beyond the scope of this book to cover the PLA's operations or their locomotives. However, it is interesting to note that a register of locomotives published in 1952, in T. B. Peacock's *PLA Railways*, lists a total of eighty-eight locos plus the three rail-motors used as replacements on the Millwall Extension.

An engine shed at the Royal Docks, with PLA locomotive No. 1276.

Gallions station in the 1930s. *Below,* a Gallions–Fenchurch Street train. At its peak the PLA's lines carried 900,000 passengers annually.

The closed Gallions station showing obvious signs of war damage, and, *below*, the interior of one of the many signal boxes on the docks.

No. 75, a typically small-wheeled 0-6-0 saddle tank built by Manning, Wardle & Co. of Leeds. *Below*, engine No. 47, an 0-4-0 built by Hudswell, Clarke & Company, also of Leeds, in 1915.

'A' signal box on the Royal Docks, 1949. *Right,* LMS advertisement for the 'new route to the Continent' via Tilbury, published in *Bradshaw's Continental Guide* in 1927. *Below,* trains and steam lorries on the Royal Victoria dock with a Blue Star liner in the background.

Engine No. 17, a saddle tank built by Alex Shanks & Sons of Arbroath for the London & India Docks Co. (*CMcC*) *Below*, a rare colour image of a PLA engine. No. 67 was an 0-6-0 side tank built by Hudswell, Clarke in 1921.

Some interesting interlopers seen at the docks: Photographed in May 1963 at Poplar Docks, BEL 1 was an electric battery-powered loco built by MotorRail in 1914. (*Tony Powell*) *Below*, an interesting pair of Austerity locomotives wrapped up for export at the exchange sidings. The number 78660 identifies it as a War Department 2-8-0, one of several sent to Hong Kong after the war. The docks handled many motor vehicles and locomotives for export were not uncommon.

The Beckton Gas Works had its own internal railway system with a stable of around forty locomotives. It wasn't a dock railway of course, but it has connections as the site was later used for the DLR's depot at Beckton. The squat engines were distinctive for their low profile and the absence of a raised cab to deal with the restricted head room in parts of the plant. The example shown above is No. 13, an 0-4-0 side tank with open cab, and according to the Beckton Works plate it was built in 1902. (*CMcC*)

Left: Beckton locos at work feeding the vast gas plant.

The saddle tanks at Beckton Gas Works were nicknamed 'Jumbos'. This is No. 21, an example of this type, No. 25, is preserved at the Bressingham Railway Museum in Diss, Norfolk. (*CMcC*)

Below, a narrow gauge locomotive used to transport workers within the Royal Arsenal, Woolwich. (*NMM*)

Appendix 1: L&BR Stations

London & Blackwall Railway

Stations – West to East	Opened	Closed	Remarks
Fenchurch Street	Aug. 1841	-	Still in use. Rebuilt in Nov. 1853. Passenger shed covered by new office development in the 1980s.
Minories	July 1840	Oct 1853	The original western terminus. From 1987 the site of Tower Gateway on the DLR.
Leman Street	June 1877	July 1941	
Cannon Street Road	Aug 1842	late 1843	
Shadwell	Oct 1840	July 1941	Renamed as Shadwell & St Georges East in 1900.
Stepney	Aug 1840	-	Renamed as Stepney East in 1923, and again as Limehouse for the DLR in 1987. Still in use.
Limehouse	July 1840	May 1926	Not to be confused with the renamed Stepney East, *above*.
West India Docks	July 1840	May 1926	
Millwall Junction	Dec 1871	May 1926	
Poplar	July 1840	May 1926	Relocated to north side of Commercial Road in 1845. Not to be confused with the DLR Poplar station.
Blackwall	July 1840	May 1926	Not to be confused with the DLR Blackwall station.

London & Blackwall Extension Railway

South to North	Opened	Closed	Remarks
Burdett Road	Sept 1871	April 1941	Damaged during Second World War air raid and fell into disuse.
Bow Road (original)	Oct 1876	April 1892	
Bow Road (replacement)	April 1892	Nov 1949	Rebuilt to north of original site.
Victoria Park & Bow	April 1849	Sept 1850	Interchange with Eastern Counties Railway whose platforms were used until 1851. Not to be confused with Victoria Park or Bow stations.

Millwall Extension Railway

North to South	Opened	Closed	Remarks
South Dock	Dec 1871	May 1926	
Millwall Docks	Dec 1871	May 1926	Sometimes shown as Millwall Docks (Glengall Road).
North Greenwich	July 1871	May 1926	Sometimes shown as North Greenwich & Cubbitt Town. Not to be confused with the present North Greenwich Underground station.

Appendix 2: L&BR Timeline

- 1836 Act of Parliament authorising the construction of The Commercial Railway.

- 1840 Line opens going from Minories to Blackwall, and the company changes its name to the London & Blackwall Railway.

- 1841 Fenchurch Street terminus and the short extension into the City of London are completed.

- 1849 The L&BR extension opens. The 5 ft ½ inch gauge is standardised and steam locomotives replace the ropes.

- 1853 Enlarged Fenchurch Street station opens.

- 1866 The L&BR is leased to the Great Eastern Railway.

- 1923 Regrouping of Britain's railways.

- 1926 Closes to passengers.

- 1948 Nationalisation of the railways.

- 1968 Remaining goods services cease.

- 1987 The Docklands Light Railway opens reusing much of the L&BR's infrastructure.

Fenchurch Street station, 2013.

Further Reading

P.L.A. Railways, by Thomas P. Peacock, Locomotive Publishing Company, 1952.
The London and Blackwall Railway, by Geoffrey Body and Robert E. Eastleigh, Trans-Rail.
Stepney's Own Railway – A History of the London & Blackwall System, by J. E. Connor, Connor & Butler, 1987.
London's Dock Railways Part 1 – The Isle of Dogs and Tilbury, by Dave Marden, Kestrel, 2012.

Other References
The Literary World: 'The London & Blackwall Railway', 7 Nov 1840.
The Leisure Hour: 'A Groat's Worth of Rail', 19 May 1843.
The Illustrated London News: 'The Camden-Town Railway', 15 Nov 1851.
   'Blackwall Extension Railway Bridge', 6 Jan 1849.
Curiosities of London, by John Timbs, 1867.
Argosy: 'To and Through the Isle of Dogs', 1867.
Dickens's Dictionary of London, by Charles Dickens (Jr), 1879.
Dickens's Dictionary of the Thames, by Charles Dickens (Jr), 1881.

Online Resources
Disused Stations – *www.disused-stations.org*
The Docklands Light Railway – *www.dlrlondon.co.uk*
Isle of Dogs – Island History Trust – *www.islandhistory.co.uk*

Acknowledgements

I would like to acknowledge and thank the many individuals and organisations who have contributed to the production of this book. Unless otherwise stated all new photography is by the author. Additional images have come from a number of sources and I am grateful to the following: The National Maritime Museum (*NMM*), the US library of Congress (*LoC*), Campbell McCutcheon (*CMcC*), John Alsop, Tony Powell2, Jonathan Whiteland, John Keogh, Tim Brown, Previnnk, and Ben Brooksbank. Special thanks to Nick Catford who produces the excellent Disused Stations website. Final thanks go to my wife, Ute Christopher. Apologies to anyone left out unknowingly and any such errors brought to my attention will be corrected in subsequent editions. *JC*